FROM THE HILL
TO THE HORIZON
1867–2017

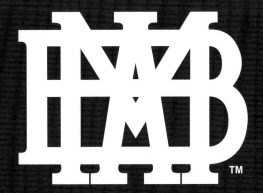

TURNER
PUBLISHING COMPANY

Montgomery Bell Academy would like to thank Tom Markham, Class of 2011, Angela Klausner, MBA Librarian, and David Ewing, MBA Fellow in the Patrick Wilson Library, and the assistance of numerous faculty and parents in collecting these images, as well as those alumni who wrote vignettes for this celebration of MBA's 150th anniversary. We have also used information from *The History of Montgomery Bell Academy* written by Ridley Wills, Class of 1952, to add context and reference to these images and perspectives.

Additionally, we are grateful to Turner Publishing, especially Jon O'Neal, and Todd Bottorff, Class of 1986, who generously supported this project.

We are indebted to these friends of MBA.

Turner Publishing Company
Nashville, Tennessee
New York, New York
www.turnerpublishing.com

From the Hill to the Horizon

Cover design: Maddie Cothren
Book design: Tim Holtz

9781683366874

Printed in the United States of America
17 18 19 20 10 9 8 7 6 5 4 3 2 1

Foreword

Our edition of From the Hill to the Horizon celebrates MBA's 150th year. In some respects, MBA was spawned from the narrows of the Harpeth River, where Montgomery Bell first built his iron forge and made his fortune. His gift of $20,000 to begin a boys school launched the MBA we know in 2017. In some ways our history goes back to the 1780's when MBA's predecessor schools first began. The images and language in this book offer a flavor of that history. We hope this book provides hours of delight for many of our friends, families, and alumni.

When I first learned about MBA in the 1970's through college classmates who had attended our school, I knew immediately that MBA was a great educational institution. Little did I realize until 1994 and these past 23 years how special, meaningful, and cherished this school community is.

I enjoy the camaraderie of a great boys school like MBA. I saw it recently at assembly when boys were connected arm-in-arm singing our alma mater. I see that spirit in those small moments early in the morning when young men are dropped off at school before 7:00 a.m. and when boys gather in the Dining Hall to enjoy breakfast with one another. I relish that spirit in the moments I witness when young men talk openly about their interests and hopes and ambitions. I see the spark in their eyes when they talk about poetry or intellectual ideas or the care and affection they have for their classmates.

MBA is a school with wonderful depth and dimension. Its ideal of Gentleman, Scholar, Athlete extends to many realms of excellence. Our students embrace all areas of the school– from the arts and all the other academic disciplines to the ways in which a debater may cheer enthusiastically for a friend on the gridiron or a young man will express his appreciation for a classmate whose excellence in music or science is spell-binding. I frequently see a kindness and gentleness in our young men that belies the world's view of young men. I am hopeful that MBA will continue to have a great influence on our city, our state, our nation, and the world. What I learned about MBA in the 1970's has proved true, but I have the conviction now that MBA will continue to be one of the great schools around the globe. May its history go on for hundreds of more years and generations of our successors build upon the work done by so many these past 150 years.

Bradford Gioia
MBA Headmaster

CAMPUS QUOTATIONS

The boys at MBA learn inside and outside of the classroom. Each building on campus contains inspiring quotations that reflect MBA's values and aspirations. These words remind us daily of the power of language and ideas. Each chapter of this book contains some of these inscriptions found on the walls or the buildings on campus.

Chapter 1

1867–1915

Iron magnate Montgomery Bell left $20,000 in his will in 1852 to establish an all-boys school in Nashville. At the time the fund was not enough to start the school, but with investments the fund grew to $45,000. In 1867 the University of Nashville started Montgomery Bell Academy on its college campus, naming it after its generous benefactor.

In 1855 Dr. John Berrien Lindsley, a medical doctor and minister, led the University of Nashville after his father, Dr. Phillip Lindsley, retired. Dr. Phillip Lindsley was

Isaac Ball
Headmaster, 1911–1942

hired in 1825 as Chancellor of the University of Nashville when he was the interim President of the College of New Jersey (now Princeton University). The elder Lindsley turned down the permanent job in New Jersey because he believed there was great potential in Nashville at the institution. It was Dr. Lindsley who originally coined the nickname "Athens of the West" (now South) for Nashville because of its educational institutions.

Tennessee was the last state to secede from the Union during the Civil War and the first to rejoin in 1866. Nashville was poised to rebound quicker than other larger Southern cities like Atlanta, Richmond, and Charleston, which were all burned during the Civil War. Nashville, founded on the banks of the Cumberland River near the location of the University of Nashville, continued to grow during this period, and the need for education increased. From 1862 to 1865, during the Civil War, no schools operated in Nashville except the University of Nashville Medical School.

Montgomery Bell Academy first opened its doors on September 9, 1867 with an enrollment of 26 boys meeting in the University of Nashville's main building. Montgomery Bell's gift to the school instructed the school to provide scholarships for boys in Nashville and the surrounding counties. A grammar school met in one classroom while the high school met in the other. The enrollment almost tripled to 74 boys by the end of the school year. During this period MBA had many principals, including J.L. Ewell (1867–1868), M.S. Snow (1868–1870), A.D. Wharton (1870–1874), Joseph W. Yeatman (1874–1886), and Samuel M. D. Clark (1886–1911).

Due to the growth of the suburbs of Nashville and convenient access to previously undeveloped areas, the Board of Trustees of MBA—who had previously split from the University of Nashville—decided to move the school in 1915. The area located between Centennial Park and Belle Meade was an ideal location that offered a spacious country environment with room to expand in the future.

Elocution First Prize Medal
1895
Presented to E.O. Dennedy

Nashville Prep School Football Champions
1900

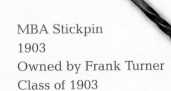

MBA Stickpin
1903
Owned by Frank Turner
Class of 1903

1867–1915

Montgomery Bell Bulletin Ad
November 1905
Describes the campus and curriculum in the early 1900s

"DO YOU SUPPOSE, WERE I YOUR FRIEND, THAT I WOULD BETRAY YOU?"

—Sam Davis

Montgomery Bell

Montgomery Bell was a successful iron foundry owner from Dickson, Tennessee. He purchased James Robertson's Cumberland Furnace and was a leader in manufacturing iron in the area. A majority of Montgomery Bell's estate paid for enslaved Africans who worked at his furnace to travel to Liberia and other countries in West Africa where they were born if they wanted to return home. The cannonballs he made helped General Andrew Jackson defeat the British in the Battle of New Orleans. At the time of his death in 1855 he left $20,000 to start a school to educate boys in the three-county area. After the end of the Civil War his gift had grown to have the funds to establish Montgomery Bell Academy at the University of Nashville.

Montgomery Bell
July 1, 1855

MBA Faculty
1909–1910
Principal S.M.D. Clark, whom the students called "Smack Me Down" Clark, is in the front row far left.

Thomas H. Malone, Jr., Class of 1886

This historic school, in that elder day (1882–1888), was a quite different affair from the urbane and polished institution known to the present generation.

The fund left by the founder, old Montgomery Bell, was for the education of 25 poor boys. The "pay" students were afterwards added under an arrangement between Professor Clark and the University of Nashville. It speaks very favorably for the democratic spirit which existed that none of us knew about the boys who were being educated on those scholarships. I never heard of scholarships until long after I left the school. While some of these boys were from the established families—there were many poverty-stricken aristocrats in the South at that time—others were definitely from parents in the humbler walks of life, boys who ordinarily would never be in a private school.

When I entered MBA the classes were held in one of the old grey buildings of the University of Nashville. The brick school house, which still stands in South Nashville, was then built, and a separate campus of some 8 or 10 acres allotted to it, and we moved in the next year.

As I recall, there were only three members of the faculty in my first year—Professor S.M.D. Clark, Professor William R. Garrett, and Professor Joseph Yeatman.

The headmaster was an old Civil War Solider, the famous S.M.D. Clark, whose initials, as successive generations of scholars had agreed, stood for "Smack-Me-Down" (as we called him in secret) and who, upon occasion, amply justified the paraphrase. Clark had a strong, resonant voice, and was an expert marksman with talc or a blackboard eraser. Whenever he would see a boy hiding behind his raised desk-lid, he would turn loose one of the blackboard rubbers, which never failed to hit the lid with a fearful crash—whereupon the surprised culprit (who was usually engaged in eating, reading a dime novel, or some other unlawful traffic) would nearly jump out of his skin. The talc or crayon was reserved for those engaged in whispering or passing notes, and the aim was equally deadly. Distance cut no figure. The extreme end of the long room was just the same as the first row of desks to him. He also had a ferule or very light paddle which was used on extreme occasions—but these were really not many. His size, his loud, strong voice, and the "steel-blue" eyes were usually sufficient to subdue the most turbulent—for he spoke as one having authority. Looking back, I can fully realize that he was one of the finest men I ever knew and led one of the most useful, honorable lives. His fixed ambition was to make boys gentlemen, even if they could not be scholars, and he did not hesitate to apply the necessary polish where it would do the most good.

Nashville, Tenn., _____ *187*

Mr E.D. Hicks *Dr.*

To the Montgomery Bell Academy,

Of the University of Nashville,

For Tuition of Gordon D Hicks *in*

HIGH SCHOOL DEPARTMENT,

for First *Quarter ending* Nov 17th *187* 0, **$20 00.**

Contingent Fee 31.00

Received Payment, Sept 8th 1880

S.M.D. Clark

Principal.

☞ *Tuition POSITIVELY payable in Advance.* ☜

Receipt for Tuition Payment
September 8, 1880
Tuition was $80 yearly for the high school and $60 for the grammar school. Stables were provided during school hours for students coming by horse and carriage.

University of Nashville

Established in 1785 as Nashville's first university, the school was eventually located up the hill on Second Avenue, north of Broadway. The school saw great growth in the mid nineteenth century, led by Dr. Phillip Lindsley, who coined the phrase "Athens of the South." The University of Nashville had an undergraduate department, a medical school, a Normal School (later Peabody College), and was where Montgomery Bell Academy was established on the campus in 1867.

University of Nashville Brochure
March 1869
Brochure from the University of Nashville,
Montgomery Bell Academy

Education after the Civil War

From 1862 to 1865 the Union Army occupied Nashville as the Confederate Army fled and left the management of the city to the Union. During this time most schools and colleges were closed, including the University of Nashville. The medical school of the university still operated due to a need for doctors to treat the injured of war. Tennessee was the last state to secede the Union and the first to rejoin after the Civil War.

Nashville was not burned during the Civil War like Richmond, Atlanta, and Charleston, and after the end of the war there was a rush to reestablish prep schools, and colleges and create new ones. Northeastern charities and religious groups helped start two African-American colleges, Fisk University and Roger Williams University, during the late 1860s. Commodore Cornelius Vanderbilt gave a gift of one million dollars to start Vanderbilt University in 1873 because the South was in need of a major college after the war.

Montgomery Bell's gift in 1852 was held and invested, and by 1867 it was large enough to open Montgomery Bell Academy at the University of Nashville.

First School Building
1881
In a block bounded by Lindsley Avenue,
Academy Place, and University Place

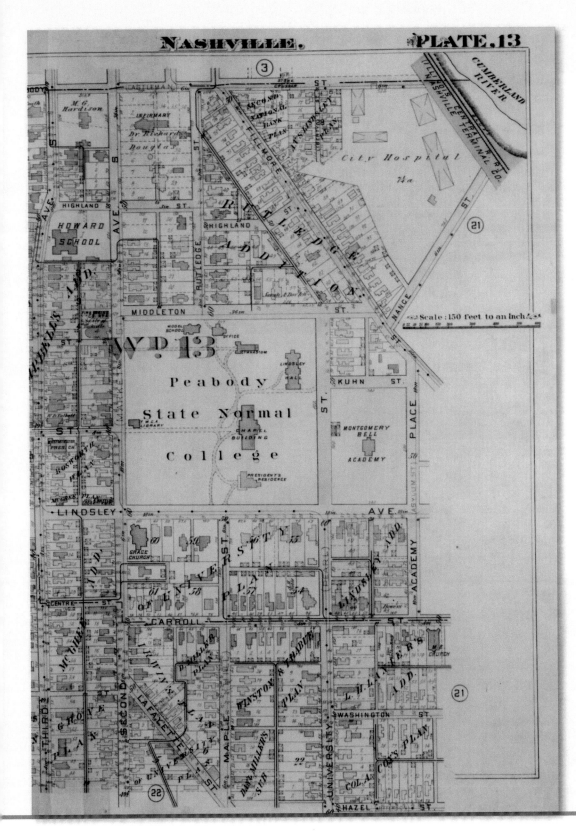

Three Downtown Locations

Montgomery Bell Academy first occupied two rooms in the main administration building of the University of Nashville. In the 1870s a separate two-story building with a three-story tower in the center was built on the campus. In 1913 MBA had to find a new home when the University of Nashville closed and the campus was in the process of being sold. MBA rented a building on 7th Avenue North just off of Charlotte, next to the State Capitol. The building with great views of the northwest part of Nashville was much larger than its previous building but still only a temporary location.

Map of Early MBA and Surrounding Area
1880s
Corner of Lindsley and Asylum Streets

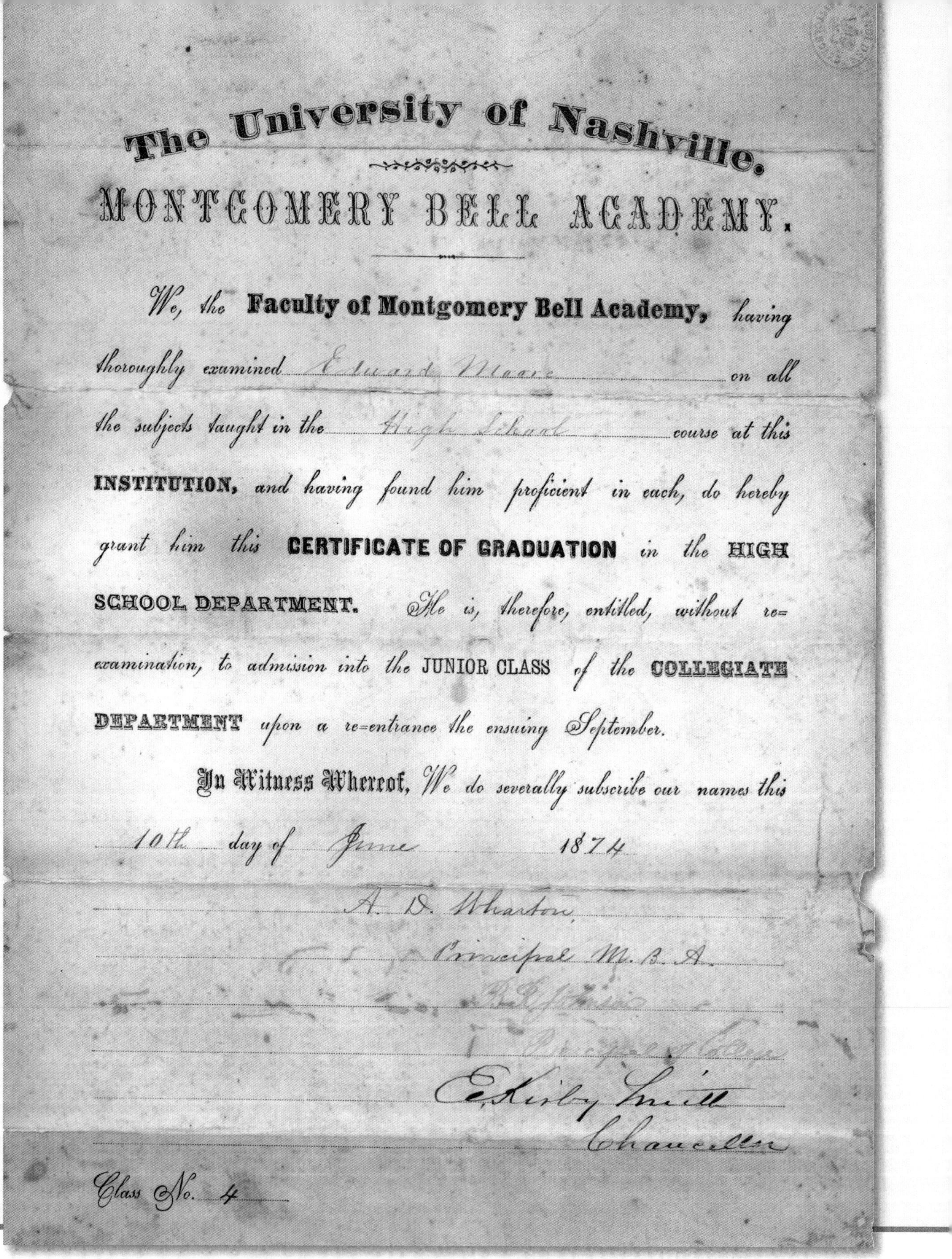

The University of Nashville.

MONTGOMERY BELL ACADEMY.

We, the **Faculty of Montgomery Bell Academy,** having thoroughly examined *Edward Moore* on all the subjects taught in the *High School* course at this **INSTITUTION,** and having found him proficient in each, do hereby grant him this **CERTIFICATE OF GRADUATION** in the **HIGH SCHOOL DEPARTMENT.** He is, therefore, entitled, without re=examination, to admission into the JUNIOR CLASS of the **COLLEGIATE DEPARTMENT** upon a re=entrance the ensuing September.

In Witness Whereof, We do severally subscribe our names this *10th* day of *June* *1874*

A. D. Wharton,

Principal M. B. A.

E. Kirby Smith

Chancellor

Class No. 4

Early Diploma
June 10, 1874
Diploma of Edward
Moore signed
by Principal
A.D. Wharton

1904 Carnegie Library Opens
Photo credit: Nashville Public Library

Lawmen with a captured moonshine still

1909 Statewide Prohibition Starts
Photo credit: University of Tennessee

1892 Union Gospel Tabernacle (Now Ryman Auditorium) Opens
Photo credit: Metro Archives

1870 Sulphur Dell Ballpark Opens
Photo credit: Metro Archives

1897 Tennessee Centennial Exposition
Photo credit: Chromolithograph by The Henderson Litho Co.

1901 National Life Insurance Founded
Photo credit: Metro Archives

1889 Electric Street Cars Replace Horse Drawn Carriages
Photo credit: Metro Archives

1871 Fisk Jubilee Singers Formed
Public Domain

1892 Joel Cheek Starts Maxwell House Coffee
Photo credit: Library of Congress

1873 Vanderbilt University Established
Photo credit: Vanderbilt University Special Collections

1912 Goo-Goo Clusters First Made
Photo credit: Standard Candy Co.

1907 First Movie Theater Opened by Tony Sudekum
Photo credit: Blog of Debbie Cox

1907 Union Station Opens
Public Domain

William Martin Award
1930
Medal for the highest honor
awarded to a student presented at
commencement to Howard Allen.

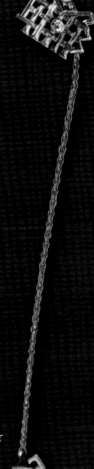

Lavalier Pin
1923
Owned by Nicholas Arthur
Wenning, Class of 1923

The 30-year period was the most challenging in MBA's history. MBA relocated its campus, Ball Hall suffered a huge fire, MBA faced a significant decline in enrollment after the stock market crash followed by the Great Depression and World War II, its longtime headmaster and visionary Issac Ball retired in 1942 after 31 years, and from 1942–1944 MBA had four different headmasters. The new campus located on the former Garland Tinsley home called "Totomoi" provided a great learning environment and land for expansion and athletic fields for a growing sports program including football, baseball, and tennis. Unemployment ran high during the Depression, and many parents could not afford to pay tuition.

In 1915 Montgomery Bell Academy left the hill overlooking the Cumberland River when the Board of Trustees voted to move to an area west of Nashville. During the Depression the Board considered selling the entire campus of the school to pay off the debt and relocate but this proposal was rejected. In 1934 the Board raised $5,000 and remained on the Harding Road campus. The school did sell surrounding land to keep the school open during the time when enrollment in most grades was in the single digits.

The Wallace School closed in 1941 when Dr. Wallace retired and the school's alumni decided to affiliate with MBA. During this time many recent graduates served the United States in World War II.

Main Building of MBA (Now the Ball Building) April 8, 1925 *Nashville Tennessean* newspaper article (photo by C.J. Burnell) of a fire that destroyed the main building, the loss being approximately $30,000

The Wallace School

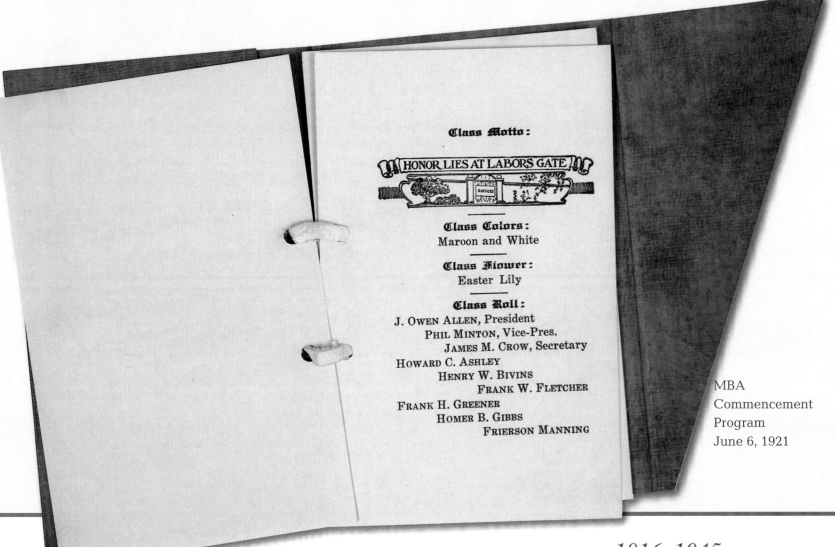

Dr. Clarence Wallace

Dr. Clarence Wallace founded an all-boys school in Nashville in 1886 called The Wallace School. The school emphasized a strong academic environment and was a rival to MBA. Wallace was never an athletic powerhouse. The schools had great respect for each other. When Dr. Wallace retired in 1941 and closed the school, the alumni decided to affiliate with MBA. The living alumni of Wallace still present a Wallace Award at MBA's commencement, and the names of all Wallace alumni are in the stairwell of the dining hall.

Class Motto:

HONOR LIES AT LABORS GATE

Class Colors:
Maroon and White

Class Flower:
Easter Lily

Class Roll:
J. OWEN ALLEN, President
PHIL MINTON, Vice-Pres.
JAMES M. CROW, Secretary
HOWARD C. ASHLEY
HENRY W. BIVINS
FRANK W. FLETCHER
FRANK H. GREENER
HOMER B. GIBBS
FRIERSON MANNING

MBA Commencement Program June 6, 1921

MBA Athletes circa 1917
Wearing beanies and an early version
of the iconic MBA waffle

First Microbe Class
1928–1929

Baseball Team on the University of Nashville Campus
Pre-1915
The school could only afford ten uniforms.

Brownlee Currey, Class of 1945

I felt that if I could get through MBA for six years, I could handle anything that came my way in life. MBA prepared me not only for college but also for life itself. Confidence was one of the strengths which the school gave me.

There are three instances that I remember distinctly.

1. I was working at Equitable Securities Corp. for one year when a gentleman asked me if I was eligible for the draft during the Korean War. I picked up the telephone and called my draft office, and this lovely woman told me I wouldn't be drafted for at least a month. Stunned, I proceeded to call on every service to see if I could get a commission as an officer. Finally the Air Force indicated I could apply for Second Lieutenant as a comptroller specialist. With confidence, I gave them all my qualifications. To make a long story short, three of us passed and the rest were dismissed. I ended up being a fighter pilot.

2. As a fighter pilot I had the confidence and courage to live through a crash. The propeller gauge went out as I came in to land, and the plane sailed over the field. I then had to put the plane down as I was only a few hundred feet over land. I saw where I wanted to put the plane down and did so. But the terrain was uneven, and the plane landed smoothly but then went up in the air before it really crashed. The engine was thrown 150 yards away, but the eight .50-caliber machine guns were still working. The rescue workers came right at me, and I had to wave them off because of fear they would fire. The crash put me in bed for two days, but then I was all right and resumed life.

3. After the Air Force I was offered a job specifically to be special assistant to the secretary of commerce in Washington. I then went on to New York and discussed the position with the executive vice president of Equitable, and he boiled it down to whether I wanted to be a politician or learn the investment banking business. It took me five minutes to decide that I wanted to learn the investment banking business. I stayed in New York for 20 years. With confidence, I accomplished many things in New York.

There you have but three instances whereby the confidence instilled in me during my years at MBA allowed me to exceed expectations. The education that I received at MBA far surpasses what can be learned from books alone.

Nashville and MBA during the Great Depression

Union Street in Downtown Nashville was known as "The Wall Street of the South" prior to the 1929 stock market crash. Locally owned Nashville banks did not panic after the crash, and Nashville did not experience the full brunt of the Great Depression until around 1932.

During this time many families' parents lost their jobs or students had to leave school to find work. Enrollment dipped at MBA to an all-time low in the mid 1930s as most graduating classes hovered around the single digits during this era. MBA was still suffering from the fire at Ball Hall in 1925.

MBA also faced its own hardship as tuition payments declined while others who attended could not pay. In 1934 MBA had a record low number of graduates in its 150-year history when only seven students received an MBA diploma. The next year in 1935 only nine students graduated, as Nashville and America were still in the grips of the Great Depression and families could not afford the tuition. Keeping the school open with low enrollment and declining funds was a challenge.

MBA Board of Trustees Secretary Brownlee O. Currey Sr. was very concerned about the finances of the school. In 1935 Currey was appointed Chairman of the Deficit Committee and was in charge of managing MBA's growing debt and keeping the school in operation. Currey was a perfect match for this role. As the co-founder of Equitable Securities Corporation based in Nashville, he understood the financial markets, investments, and debt. *During this time Currey's stewardship managing the school's debt during the height of the Great Depression and contributing much-needed funds kept the doors of the school open when it lacked the finances to operate.*

"SOMETIMES QUESTIONS ARE MORE IMPORTANT THAN ANSWERS."
—Nancy Willard

M. B. A. to Continue.

There have been disquieting rumors this year with regard to the future of Montgomery Bell Academy.

It was said there was a likelihood that this school, which has made such a valuable contribution to the education of Nashville boys, might not be able to open its doors next fall, and there was even talk that the property on Harding Road might be acquired by the city for use as a high school.

The passing of this institution would be nothing short of a tragedy. It numbers among its graduates many of the most civic-minded leaders among the men of Nashville. The boys who attend M. B. A. go out from it into college or into the workaday world better equipped to make splendid records.

It was with a great measure of satisfaction, therefore, to read in Wednesday morning's newspaper that M. B. A. has weathered its financial worries and will open in the fall as usual.

Judge Thomas H. Malone, Jr., chairman of the school's board, announced following a board meeting Tuesday afternoon that the decision to reopen, encouraged by the fact that for the past three years the school had been making steady progress out of its difficulties, was unanimous.

There is a very definite place for such institutions as Montgomery Bell Academy in the Nashville scheme. They impart an education in the broader sense of the word. Unhampered by too severe standardization, or by enrollment so great that the individual is swallowed up by numbers, a school of that type gives the pupil the advantage of a more personal contact with his teachers than he might obtain in a larger school, and the precept of an educator of fine character is more directly imparted to him.

M. B. A. has made, throughout the depression, a courageous fight to keep going, and it is a matter for congratulation to the entire community that it has at last scored a definite victory.

MBA to Continue School Operations
June 2, 1935
Nashville Tennessean newspaper article about MBA's fight to keep its doors open during the Depression.

Joe Thompson, Wallace Class of 1937
circa 1940
during World War II

War Comes to MBA

After Japan bombed Pearl Harbor and the United Stated entered World War II, many students and recent graduates signed up for the service. At the time a man had to be 18 years old to serve, but many people who were under age said they were 18 in order to serve.

Although not a military school, the skills learned at MBA were in demand in the service, and many MBA graduates served their country with honor.

Outside the Wilson Library, MBA has recognized their graduates who have paid the ultimate sacrifice with markers of their names from World War I, World War II, Korea, and Vietnam wars.

Dwight D. Eisenhower and Winston Churchill
Photo credit: Joe Thompson, Wallace Class of 1937

General Frank Maxwell Andrews

Born in Nashville on February 3, 1884, Frank Andrews graduated from MBA in 1901 and immediately enrolled at United States Military Academy at West Point, where he graduated in 1906. A career military officer, Andrews served in World War I and World War II and quickly rose through the ranks.

During World War II President Franklin Roosevelt named Andrews to lead and to help improve the air corp prior to the United States entering the war.

At the time of his death, General Andrews was the commander of all Allied Forces in Europe and the highest ranking officer of the Allied force to die in the line of duty. General Andrews is buried in Section 3 of Arlington National Cemetery. Andrews Air Force Base (now Joint Base Andrews), the home of Air Force One, is named in his honor.

General Frank M. Andrews
February 5, 1943
Nashville Banner newspaper article "Nashvillian Heads European Command"

The Honor System
1945
Three typed pages of Honor System guidelines and rules. Includes information about "pledging" papers and tests. Also includes 20 "Points to Stress" to the students. Of interest … #11 Leave water pistols, knives, pea shooters, and chewing gum at home. #13 Rise when a guest or lady enters the room. #17 … do not write on desks … tops or bottoms … no ink at school.

THE HONOR SYSTEM

In 1945 the student body of Montgomery Bell Academy, in order to promote among its members a strong sense of certain ideals associated with gentlemanly conduct, adopted the Honor System.

Briefly stated, the code defines such conduct as follows:

> 1. Each M.B.A. boy is a person of honor who will not lie, cheat, or steal.

> 2. Desiring the good name of the school to be upheld, an M.B.A. student is unwilling to have as a member of the student body a boy who is dishonorable.

Other important aspects of the Honor System are these:

> 1. On all tests and examinations, each student is required to sign the following pledge: "I have neither given nor received aid on this work". (It is, of course, a violation to give assistance on pledged work.)

> 2. The Honor Council, composed of twelve boys elected by their classmates, acts as a court of honor in handling matters presented to it.

> 3. The school will not retain a boy who is persistently dishonorable.

M.B.A. has a great heritage from the past, and wishes to maintain the place it holds in the esteem of its alumni and friends; therefore, it asks each student to do his best to uphold the Honor System.

MBA Students
circa 1928

Microbes
1940

Howard Allen and His Basketball Team
1939
Mid-South Champs won 22 lost 2

In Nashville History

1942 Nashville's First Music
Publisher Acuff-Rose

Photo credit: The Conservancy for the
Parthenon & Centennial Park

1936 Berry Airport Opens

Photo credit: The Nashville International Airport

1937 African-American
Tennessee Artist William
Edmonson Show in NYC

Public Domain

1925 Grand Ole Opry

Photo credit: Nashville Public Library
Digital Collections

1933 Tornado Hits East Nashville

Photo credit: Nashville Weather Service

1916 East Nashville Fire

Photo credit: Metro Archives

1941 Iroquois Steeplechase Inaugural Race

Photo credit: The *Nashville Tennessean*

1945 VJ Day Celebration

Photo credit: Metro Archives

1918 Dutchman's Curve Train Crash

Photo credit: The *Nashville Tennessean*

1927 Warner Parks Open

Photo credit: Licensed under
Creative Commons

Chapter 3

1946–1957

Students on Campus
1947

The post-World War II years at MBA saw increased enrollment and more stability in the headmaster's position as Robert Sager led the school from 1944 to 1957. There were 214 boys enrolled in the school in the fall of 1945. The first edition of The Bell, the MBA yearbook, was published in 1945.

Nashville enjoyed a post-war boom, and the downtown area where MBA was founded experienced a renaissance. Future MBA Board member Guilford Dudley, Jr. constructed the Life & Casualty Tower, the tallest building in the South in 1957.

Totomoi

In February of 1954, Inman Fox and Bob McNeilly Jr., both 1950 graduates, organized a society named Totomoi to honor MBA students who made outstanding contributions in scholarship, student government, publications, athletics, and organizations.

The name "Totomoi" was the name of the home of the Tinsley family before MBA purchased the grounds and the building today known as "Ball Hall." Each year students and occasionally alumni and faculty members are selected to join the society during a special ceremony. Today this society is still the highest honor a boy can achieve.

First Totomoi Inductees
Class of 1954
Seawall Brandau,
Robert Colton Jr.,
Robert Lightfoot Jr.,
Robert Lineberger,
William Pfeiffer Jr.,
Carlin Rolfe,
John Sloan Jr.,
Stephen Wood

Mothers and Students
1956

"YESTERDAY IS HISTORY. TOMORROW IS A MYSTERY.
TODAY IS A GIFT. THAT IS WHY IT IS CALLED THE PRESENT."
—Eleanor Roosevelt

Robert E. McNeilly Jr., Class of 1950

What did MBA mean to me starting in 1946? Solidifying friendships into intimate "best friend" status; learning under several gifted teachers who prepared me well: McCandles, Lowry, Sager, Wise; success in athletics and experiencing the power of team. Then seeing the MBA experience grow from strength to strength. So proud!

"THE TEST OF A GOOD TEACHER IS NOT HOW MANY QUESTIONS HE CAN ASK HIS PUPILS THAT THEY WILL ANSWER READILY, BUT HOW MANY QUESTIONS HE INSPIRES THEM TO ASK HIM WHICH HE FINDS IT HARD TO ANSWER."

—Alice Wellington Rollins

Paul Harmon, Class of 1957

My wife, Karen Roark, once Chair of the English Department at The Harpeth Hall School, commented that all my old MBA alumni friends have a uniquely active interest in poetry. I believe that to be true, and I attribute this one love of verse to our English teacher, Miss Bitzer (after her marriage, Mrs. Lowry to later students).

With a book in one hand and a heavy staff in the other, she walked around the classroom reading "The Telltale Heart" by Edgar Allan Poe while keeping a heartfelt cadence by heavy pounding of the staff on the wood floor. I'm sure, at the time, neighboring classrooms got a reverberating taste of that poem and now, nearly six decades later, I clearly hear that telltale heart, and so much more.

This is one of so many examples I could relate to illustrate the point: that's what great teachers and great schools like MBA do. They open doors to treasures to use and enrich us for the rest of our lives.

East High vs. MBA Football Program
1952
Wayne Renegar, Head Coach

Nashville Banner Banquet of Champions
January 31, 1956
Featuring football players Frank
Burkholder (Class of 1956), Tom Husband
(Class of 1957), Mack Rolfe (Class of 1956),
and Russell Brothers (Class of 1957)

Rildley Wills II, Class of 1952

My memories of MBA are fresh and positive. Despite the fact that I was not a strong student, my teachers at MBA left me well prepared for Vanderbilt, where I and most of my classmates matriculated. I particularly cherish the friendships I made at MBA. Many of my classmates became lifelong friends. In looking at the pictures of my 36 classmates, I felt our class was exceptional. We had seven or eight extraordinary students, five of whom became physicians.

Playing on the varsity football and basketball teams was very valuable to me. On the playing field, I learned the importance of teamwork. I had grown up in the very privileged Belle Meade neighborhood and had, before coming to MBA in the ninth grade, little exposure to boys from less advantaged neighborhoods. However, in competing with boys from such schools as Gallatin, West, Father Ryan, Isaac Litton, and Springfield, in both basketball and football, I realized I could compete with them. That was surprising and satisfying.

I have vivid memories of our 12 dedicated teachers, one of whom was our headmaster, Dr. Richard Lee Sager. My favorite was his wife, who taught Spanish, a subject I enjoyed. I particularly remember Mrs. Sager for her kindness.

MBA in 1952 had only three buildings—the main building (now Ball Hall), a gymnasium, and a science and math building. If you count the springhouse, we had four. Nevertheless, I never heard a classmate complain about our limited facilities, even though we did complain about the food in our basement cafeteria.

I am certainly proud of MBA's magnificent facilities today, but I have long realized that great teachers are more important than facilities.

"WE MAKE A LIVING BY WHAT WE GET,
BUT WE MAKE A LIFE BY WHAT WE GIVE."
—Winston Churchill

Richard Porter, Class of 1950

I am deeply grateful to MBA for all it has given me, to my son, Kirk Porter, and to my grandsons, Andrew Porter and William Porter. This poem was read at our 50th class reunion in 2000.

Can these men on the threshold of age, their careers largely
Behind them, have played their hearts out on Andrews Field?
Can those tousled kids with little mind for money
Be these tycoons who maximize their yield?

Can these churchmen, these icons, these patrons of all worthwhile
Have parked in Percy Warner to explore their date?
Can they have angered Cremo, drawn demerits,
And passed their roguish teen years tempting fate?

Can men who have copied with all the trials of life
Have struggled no less for Hackman, Bitzer and Rule?
Can boys who differed inside as much as boys could
Have been united by the magic of a school?

It can be and is, every word true. What wonders
May yet await only time will tell.
With fifty years of gratitude, we thank you,
Alma Mater. God Bless You Montgomery Bell.

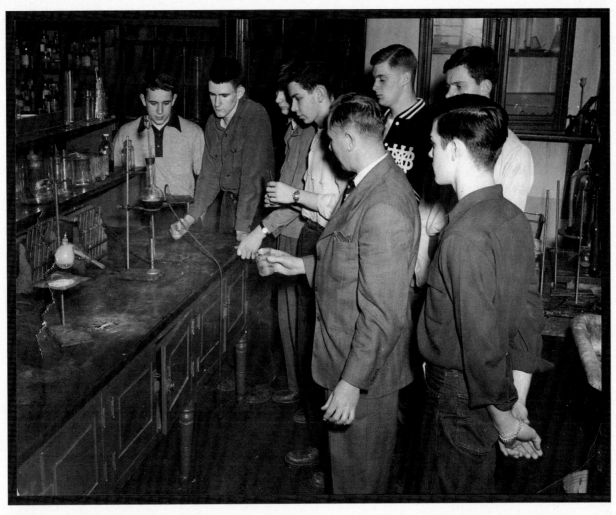

Chemistry Class
1949–1950
Taught by Henry Hackman

"I HAVE NOT FAILED. I'VE JUST FOUND
10,000 WAYS THAT DON'T WORK."
—Thomas Edison

"STRIVE MIGHTILY, BUT EAT AND DRINK AS FRIENDS."
—William Shakespeare

Spring Prom
1953

The Register

Signing the register has been part of the school's heritage since 1844, (originally started at the Western Military Institute which later merged with the University of Nashville). The large register book is maintained in the archives of the Wilson Library. By signing the register each year, these gentlemen, scholars, and athletes not only join the Long Red Line of men who preceded them but also pledge to support the school's honor code, which is printed in large letters on the top of every page of the register.

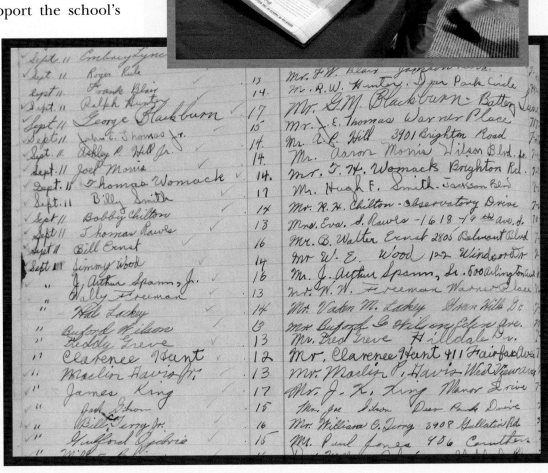

1957 L & C Tower Built
Photo credit: Image Courtesy of Jeff Nixon

1950 WSM-TV Established
Photo credit: WSM

1951 Belmont College Opens
Photo credit: US GenWeb Archives

1951 Harpeth Hall School Founded
Photo credit: Private School Review

1950 Approximately 10,500 Tennesseans Served in the
Korean War
Photo credit: Dept. of Veteran Affairs, National Cemetery
Administration

Chapter 4

1957–1978

Headmaster Francis E. Carter
June 1967

Francis Carter was hired as headmaster and joined the school in 1957. The popular headmaster led the school during a time of population growth in Nashville and conflict in America involving the Civil Rights Movement and the Vietnam War. During his time Currey Gymnasium opened as well as Wallace Hall.

MBA graduate Nelson Andrews led the efforts to help pass liquor by the drink in Nashville, which increased the city's restaurants, taxes, and tourism.

Mary Helen Lowry

Mrs. Lowry was a fixture at MBA who taught English for 50 years, and every student she taught emerged as a better and more articulate writer. After her death in 1998, she was posthumously elected a member of the 2002 Tennessee Teachers Hall of Fame. MBA honored this longtime faculty member by naming the newest academic building on The Hill "Lowry Hall," which opened in 2012.

English Teacher Mary Helen Lowry
1970s

Spaghetti Supper

In the fall of 1946, the Women's Auxiliary established a long-standing tradition by sponsoring MBA's first spaghetti supper. Every MBA student participates in the annual fundraiser for the school by selling tickets to their family, friends, and MBA alumni. The popular annual event of the spaghetti supper packs the Currey Gym before the homecoming game and now even includes the option of take-out orders.

Spaghetti Supper Chairs
October 3, 1966

Tommy Owen,
Head Football
Coach and
History Teacher
1969

"CHARACTER IS MUCH EASIER KEPT THAN RECOVERED."
—Thomas Paine

William H. Frist,
future U.S. Senate
Majority Leader
1964–1965
on the far right, as
a seventh grader

M.B.A. HIGH SCHOOL
BOOK LIST 1965-66

<u>Grade</u>   <u>Price</u>

<u>ENGLISH</u>

9   <u>Word Wealth</u>, W. S. Miller, 1958 ed. . . . .$ 3.50
9   <u>Great Short Stories</u>, Schramm, 1950 ed. 3.00
9   <u>Huckleberry Finn</u>, Norton Critical Edition (paperback) . 1.95
9   <u>Poetry, a Closer Look</u>, Reid, Ciardi, Perrine 1.50
9   <u>Richard III</u>, Folger edition (paperback) 45
9   <u>McGraw-Hill Handbook of English</u>, Shaffer & Shaw, 1960 . . 3.65
9   <u>The Illiad of Homer</u>, translated by Lattimore (paperback) 1.95
9   <u>M.B.A. Directory</u> (Ladies Aux. to deliver) 50

10   <u>Heath Handbook of English</u> (complete course), 1961 ed.
         Christ, Starkey, Tressler **2.35**
10   <u>Words and Ideas</u>, Didas 85
10   <u>Adventures in American Literature</u>, Fuller & Kinnick,
         Laureate Edition, 1963 . . . . 4.90
10   Thoreau: <u>Walden</u>, a Writer's Edition with Commentaries
         and Notes by Larzer Ziff 2.50
10   <u>The Red Badge of Courage</u>: Crane, edited by Lettis,
         McDonald and Morris 2.15
10   <u>Word Wealth</u>, W. S. Miller, 1958 ed. 3.50
10   <u>M.B.A. Directory</u> (Ladies Aux. to deliver) 50

11   <u>English Grammar & Composition</u> (complete course) 1957,
         by Warriner and Griffith 3.60
11   <u>Adventures in English Literature</u>, Priestley, Spear &
         Bowman, Laureate edition, 1963 ed. 4.90
11   Thoreau: <u>Walden</u>, a Writer's Edition with Commentaries &
         Notes by Larzer Ziff 2.50
11   <u>Arms and the Man</u>: Shaw (paperback edition) 50
11   <u>The Importance of Being Earnest</u>, Wilde (paperback) 95
11-H <u>An Enemy of the People</u>, Ibsen (paperback) 60
11   <u>M.B.A. Directory</u> (Ladies Aux. to deliver) 50
11-12 <u>College Entrance Reviews in English Composition</u>, Orgel 1.95
11-12 <u>College Entrance Reviews in English Aptitude</u>, Orgel . . 1.95

High School Book List
1965–1966

Joseph W. Prueher, Class of 1960

The transition from Headmaster Sager to Carter. Large culture shift with effective enhancement of "Gentleman, Scholar, Athlete." Mr. Carter's characterization of Alexander Hamilton's defining outlook that "the people are a great beast" has always stuck with me. Bad lunches. Tired physical plant which seemed not to affect adversely the quality of education. Mr. Carter's energy and zeal to make MBA excellent.

Coach Owen. His influence on generations is manifest. A particular memory is our asking him (in the midst of a hard-fought game with Father Ryan) how to respond to foul play in the pile after a tackle.

He said to play by the rules but to "humiliate 'em." Strong advice for many situations.

Mrs. Lowry (then Ms. Bitzer). Like so many others I recall her demanding enthusiasm, commitment to excellence, and fair treatment of all, leavened by her marvelous competence, as being one of the main pillars of MBA.

The sometimes latent talent of classmates. Not so much in the arts in our day. Particularly think of Alex Porter, whose quiet gifts came to the fore as he became one of the foremost sprinters MBA, then Vanderbilt and the SEC, ever had. Seeing Porter, Pickel, Moss, and Hardison run sprint relays is somehow etched in my mind. Those guys could fly.

"LET HONOR BE TO US AS STRONG AN OBLIGATION AS NECESSITY IS TO OTHERS."
—Pliny the Elder

STUDENT COUNCIL CONSTITUTION
OF M. B. A.

ARTICLE 1

Functions:

A. to provide a forum for student expression through which each student while at Montgomery Bell Academy may contribute of his own thought and service to the continuous improvement of the school

B. to serve as a liaison between the Student Body and the Faculty as an effective representative of the desires and wishes of all students by serving wherever possible as an advisory committee on student policies

C. to encourage a sense of responsibility among the students for understanding, appreciating, and helping to maintain and perpetuate the fine traditions and noble ideals of Montgomery Bell Academy

ARTICLE 2

Rules:

Every student shall be a gentleman on and off campus as interpreted by the Student Council and/or the Administration.

ARTICLE 3

Organization and Membership:

A. The Student Council shall be composed of the class officers of each grade in the High School as well as a representative of the Junior School.

B. The Senior Class president shall be head of the Student Council and shall call and preside over all Student Council meetings.

C. The Senior Class vice-president shall take the place of the president in his absence.

D. The Senior Class secretary shall keep accurate minutes of all Student Council meetings.

E. The Senior Class treasurer shall handle all money matters of the Student Council in cooperation with the financial secretary of the school.

F. The presidents of the Ninth, Tenth, Eleventh, and Twelfth Grades shall make up an Executive Committee of the Student Council whose duties shall be to plan and call meetings, investigate students to be brought up before the Council, and to present their findings to the Council for any action to be taken.

G. In any case pertaining to a seventh grader or an eighth grader, the three class officers from his classroom shall meet with the Student Council and each shall have a vote in the proceedings.

ARTICLE 4

Election of Members:

A. The officers of each class shall consist of a president, a vice-president, a secretary, and a treasurer.

B. The officers of each class shall be elected in order of importance as stated above by a majority of the number of those students voting.

C. During the first week in May, the elections will be held for those officers who will assume their respective positions the following September, in all cases except the Freshman Class and the Junior School. The Freshman Class officers and the Junior School officers shall be elected at an appropriate time near the beginning of the school year.

D. In order to qualify for election to a particular office, a candidate must have passed at least four academic subjects for the first semester and must have gathered a nominating petition of at least twenty valid signatures from members of his class. Petitions shall be turned in to the office no later than Friday of the week preceding the elections.

E. The nominees for each office shall be posted by the school office for inspection, and time for delivering relevant speeches will be allotted to each candidate. Secret ballots will then be cast in the following manner; on the ballot, each student shall list, in order of preference, the candidates for a particular office. The senior Student and Honor Council officers will then count the first-place votes; the candidate garnering the lowest first-place vote total shall be eliminated. The second preference of a ballot whose first-place choice has been eliminated will then be counted as a first-place vote. This process shall continue until all but one of the candidates have been eliminated. The remaining candidate will then be declared the winner. If an elected officer does not become a member of his class, a special election will be held the next year to fill this office.

F. The Junior School representative to the Student Council shall be a member of the Eighth-grade Class elected at large by the members of both the Seventh and Eighth-grade Classes.

ARTICLE 5

Duties:

A. The Student Council shall meet whenever deemed necessary by the Executive Committee, Student Council president, or the Headmaster.

B. The Student Council shall cooperate with the Headmaster and Faculty, by investigating infractions of school policies concerning matters of dress, language, and behavior and by taking action on these matters by meeting and recommending penalties to the Headmaster by a two-thirds majority of all the members of the Student Council, for it is understood that executive authority is lodged with the Headmaster.

C. The Student Council may suggest various projects and activities that the clubs of Montgomery Bell Academy may undertake.

D. The Student Council shall encourage interest in activities, such as the annual spaghetti supper, faculty-student athletic contests, and assembly programs.

ARTICLE 6

Ratification and Amending Process:

A. This Student Council Constitution will go into effect immediately upon receiving a three-fourths majority vote of the Student Council, a two-thirds majority vote of the Student Body, majority vote of the Faculty, and final approval by the Headmaster.

B. An amendment to this Constitution proposed by any student or faculty member may be presented to the Student Council for consideration. This Constitution may be so amended by a three-fourths majority vote of the Student Council, by a two-thirds majority vote of the Student Body, by a majority vote of the Faculty, and by final approval of the Headmaster.

January 1, 1969
Revised September, 1973
Revised May, 1977

Student Council Constitution
May 1977
Original in 1969, revised in 1973
and 1977

The Blue Guitar

The Blue Guitar
1974
MBA's first literary magazine, this issue includes original works by well-known MBA alums and artists Alan LeQuire (Class of 1974) and Paul Harmon (Class of 1957).

THE WHITE HOUSE

WASHINGTON

TO THE GRADUATING CLASS
MONTGOMERY BELL ACADEMY, 1967

Please accept my warm congratulations upon your successful completion of high school. I know the pride your families and friends feel on this occasion, and I share it.

You and I cherish the same American ideals -- ever larger freedoms, ever brighter opportunity for individual fulfillment for our citizens and for all mankind. We share the continuing task of perpetuating these ideals and translating them into reality. It is not my job alone, nor yours alone. It is ours together.

No one realizes more than your President that success will depend in large measure upon the priceless legacy you carry away from these halls: the knowledge you have won here; the stronger and more certain faith in yourselves that has been born here.

I want you to know that there is no finer contribution you can make for your country than to continue your adventure in education.

In this era of growing complexity and advancing technology, our country can remain strong and prosperous only when each young American acquires all the education he can possibly absorb.

You have my every best wish for a lifetime of success and achievement.

Sincerely,

Lyndon B. Johnson

Letter to Graduates from
President Lyndon Johnson
May 1967 in honor of
MBA's 100th anniversary

Tupper Saussy's English Class
1958–1959
This flamboyant teacher's eccentricities were fodder for
Sam Pickering Jr.'s *Dead Poets Society*.

Anderson Gaither, Faculty, 1971–2014

In my life have occurred two unbelievably fortunate events. The first came upon me in March of 1971 when Mr. Carter offered me a job at MBA. The school was not all unknown to me, for I had grown up on Brighton Road (in a house since demolished to create the new tennis courts), and I had had several cousins and uncles attend MBA. Just hearing about the school, however, did not reveal what the school actually is. You have to be totally a part of the experience to understand the beauty and the dedication and the tradition which create the environment that is MBA.

Over the years there have been for the school two constants: change and an everlasting essence. The infrastructure and the technology at MBA have continually evolved and are as modern as any school in the country, but the essence of MBA remains beautifully the same. When I started at MBA, there was a quonset hut with a weight machine and a wrestling mat where now stands the auxiliary gym, there was no Massey Building and the junior school classrooms were in the Ball Building, the cafeteria was in the basement of the Ball Building, and the science labs were in the basement of the gym with no new science building. There was no Davis Building or theater, only a service road where the arts now prevail, Wallace Hall had only recently been converted from a gym and now has been replaced by a fabulous dining facility; moreover, my classroom of 41 years on the first floor of old Wallace had once been a dressing room, there was no track and no soccer field and no wrestling room, and German and Chinese were not in the curriculum.

Though so much about MBA has indeed changed and though the faces and names on campus are different each year, never really changing are the young, diffident boys entering the school tentatively and leaving as confident young men; never really changing are the parents who come to love the school and to support it long after their sons graduate; never really changing (since the 1970s, anyway) is the Board of Trustees which respects and understands the needs of a world-class academy; and never really changing, except at the edges, is the curriculum which reflects the ideals of a classical education in a modern world.

When I look back over my 43 years at MBA, I may have forgotten some names, but I can actually still see the faces of so many of my students sitting in class, trying their best to learn Latin. I can still see my wrestlers who worked harder than I could ever have worked myself. I can still see my track runners doing one or two laps beyond what they felt possible, just because they had pride in themselves and in their school. I can still see the faces of the diligent writers and editors for the school newspaper staying up late into the night to meet a deadline, producing articles of genuine interest for me to proofread. MBA brings forth something in these teenage boys which makes them want to work hard, brings forth a determination to succeed and to be so proudly a part of the greatness which is MBA.

Even two years into retirement, I feel so lucky to have shared a classroom with the legendary Coach Owen, to have chatted frequently with the equally legendary Mrs. Lowry, whose room was just down the hall from mine, to have been a close colleague and friend with Dr. Gaffney, a man of immense talent and capacity, to have coached and taught with the remarkable Mike Drake, who held almost every job at MBA, to have read Caesar and Cicero and Vergil and Ovid with so many fascinating students, each one uniquely interesting. And, with just as much good fortune have I worked under four remarkably talented and devoted headmasters: Mr. Carter, who would arrive at 4:00 A.M. to ensure that the furnaces

were working and who, in his paternalistic manner, brought a bit more discipline to the student body; Mr. Bondurant, who convinced others of the need for more money to be spent for the faculty and for the grounds and buildings and who reminded the teachers that every moment we are with our students is precious; Dr. Paschall, who with Ridley Wills saw the need to increase the presence of the arts on campus and in the curriculum; and especially Mr. Gioia, who has made MBA into a truly international presence, has broadened tremendously the alumni involvement both financially and emotionally, and who has been a true friend to me and to so many during his time at MBA.

I wish I could list all the students and colleagues who have made a huge impression on me and on the school, but space demands an abbreviation. I learned early on that teaching is as much the interaction of personalities as it is the art of imparting knowledge, and there have been some real personalities here over the years. I have loved MBA from the first day on the job because it was so fulfilling to work in this environment where everyone also loves the school and its essential goodness.

English Teacher June Bowen
in the late 1970s

"KEEP YOUR EYES ON THE STARS AND YOUR FEET ON THE GROUND."
—Theodore Roosevelt

JESSE
HILL
FORD
1976

Jesse Hill Ford's Edgar Award
1976
The Edgar Award (named after
Edgar Allan Poe) was presented
by The Mystery Writers of
America to honor Jesse Hill
Ford, Class of 1947, for his short
story "The Jail."

Championship Pennant
1967
Class AAA Football Title

"FOR MY PART I KNOW NOTHING WITH ANY CERTAINTY,
BUT THE SIGHT OF THE STARS MAKES ME DREAM."
—Vincent van Gogh

Marc K. Stengel, Class of 1974

I cannot recall that I have ever not been proud—and indeed grateful—to have been associated with Montgomery Bell Academy for what now amounts to over 45 years. This is not to say that I have conveniently forgotten the serial anguish any student feels over continual testing and writing and note taking and presentation making. When these activities are in the present, they can be bloodcurdling; but through the golden veil of memory they are fondly missed while facing later, more adult challenges outside of the supportive embrace of faculty, coaches, and staff—and, yes, even trustees—who have always constituted the essential nature of MBA to my mind. If I were asked at this stage of an eventful and adventuresome life just what I felt I have chiefly gained from my "experience" of MBA,

I would not hesitate to say it is Independence of Outlook. Valuable as they have been, the fruits of my studies were absorbed (and savored) from without; durable friendships were formed and enjoyed in extroverted groups; but the independence of thought and behavior that I consider chief among my blessings in life was craftily coaxed from within me (and often without an awareness of such) by the various personalities who once peopled my world as defined by the geographical limits of life on MBA's campus. It makes me smile inwardly to this day when I consider that "his damnable independence" was undoubtedly an unintended consequence of most of my encounters with the denizens of MBA in the early 1970s, but I pocked that windfall just the same, and I have cherished it uppermost amongst all of the other treasures of my memories of my time at Montgomery Bell Academy.

Name Badges
1967
From MBA's
100th Anniversary
(1867–1967)

Tuition through the Ages

Montgomery Bell's will instructed that students to attend MBA from Davidson and five surrounding counties free of charge. In the 1880s, due to the growth of the school and demand to enroll, a paid tuition program was also established.

Financial Statement of Butch Smith, Class of 1966

BUTCH

STUDENT'S NAME   STATEMENT

MONTGOMERY BELL ACADEMY
HARDING ROAD
NASHVILLE, TENNESSEE 37205

- MR. TRUETT K. SMITH
  4606 BELMONT PARK TERRACE
  NASHVILLE, TENNESSEE

To Insure Proper Credit Return This Stub

DATE		FOLIO	CHARGES	CREDITS	BALANCE
9/1/65	Tuition		650.		
	Activity Fee		25.		
	Laboratory Fee				
	Graduation Fee				
	Entry Fee Credit			25.	650.
	Graduation fee		10.		660.

TUITION IS DUE IN ADVANCE

Alma Mater

In 1957, several members of the Alumni Association persuaded songwriters Beasley Smith and Ralph Freed to write an alma mater for MBA. The trustees voted to accept it as the official school song, a decision that was later ratified by a vote of the student body.

Hail MBA of thee we sing
Now and forever more.
Long may the bells of glory ring,
As in the days of yore.
Hail to thee! Hail to thee!
Where loyal hearts and friendship dwell.
On and On! Faithfully,
Hail Montgomery Bell!

Alma Mater

Steven M. Zager, Class of 1976

Selma Ridgway gave me my first legal pad more than 43 years ago. Little did I know then that legal pads would be my constant companions. In those days, MBA was yet to become the debate powerhouse that it is today. We sold chocolate almond candy bars and golf shirts to finance our bus trips to tournaments. Joanne Armour, a parent, volunteered as our only assistant coach. We travelled many weekends to tournaments in places like Selma, Alabama, and Larue County, Kentucky. Most did not really understand or appreciate our sacrifices, or so I thought.

Steven Eisen and I were fortunate to win the National Bicentennial Debate Championship in Philadelphia in 1976. The final debate was held in Independence Hall. In those days, it was customary to present trophies for championships to Mr. Carter and the school in a morning assembly. We did. Mr. Carter accepted the trophy and commented that it was almost as good as winning a state wrestling championship. We were disappointed in Mr. Carter's comments. But, here is the thing about MBA. Before the week was out, just about every athlete in our class sought me out to tell me that Mr. Carter was wrong and that a "national" debate championship made them proud of us and proud of MBA.

MBA is so much more than a campus on a hill. MBA is students who care about one another in profound ways. Many of those athletes are still my closest friends today.

"HONOR - YOUR WORD IS YOUR BOND. TRUTH, HONESTY, AND CHARACTER ARE YOUR WATCHWORDS NEVER TO BE FORGOTTEN."
—Colin Powell

Patrick Hale Memorial Golf Tournament

Patrick Hale, Class of 1992, was tragically killed in a hit-and-run accident in New York in 2003. His father, Walter Hale (Class of 1961), family, and friends organized an annual golf tournament in his honor. Since 2003 the Patrick Hale Fund has raised over $1,000,000 to benefit MBA. Walter Hale says, "The Patrick Hale Fund is about investing in young men to give them the values and qualities that will influence them over a lifetime."

Patrick Hale Golf Tournament

1963 Metropolitan Government Formed
Photo credit: Nashville Public Library Digital
   Collections

1960 Nashville Civil Rights Protests
Photo credit: Metro Archives

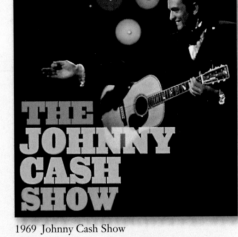

1969 Johnny Cash Show
Photo credit: Internet Movie Database

1961 Country Music Hall of Fame
Established
Photo credit: The Country Music Hall of
   Fame

1969 Hee Haw Television Show
Photo credit: Oklahoma History Center

1972 Opryland USA Opens
Photo credit: Tennessee Concerts

Chapter 5

1979–1988

Gordon Bondurant became headmaster in 1979. The campus expanded again with MBA Board member Jack Massey's gift, establishing a new building for the Junior School. Enrollment of the school grew as well as the population of the city.

Headmasters Douglas Paschall (1988–1989)
and Gordon Bondurant (1979–1988)
circa 1988

Football Cheerleaders
1979

The MBA experience contains defining moments created by legendary people.

Art Department Chairman
Jim Womack
1979

March 1980

Is it the soft yellow of the jonquil against the rich green leaf, or is it the melodious sound of a multitude of chirping birds? Is it the crack of a baseball slamming into a baseball bat, or is it the brightly colored tennis racquet covers strewn about the court? Is it the pointed smell of freshness in the air, or is it the warm breeze that greets the unexpected? Whatever it is, Spring is beginning to show unmistakable signs of arriving. Linda and I purchased a front-wheel drive car and viciously-studded tires for another car in order to be prepared for the onslaught of a Nashville winter. Behold, it never arrived! Spring brings new life to us all, and it is no more abundantly evident than within the MBA community.

As you will understand when you have completed reading this publication, MBA is alive with activity in the next two months. We invite your participation in as many of these functions as you can possibly attend. I can promise you much fun and excitement around an enthusiastic group of young men.

MBA and HARPETH HALL JOIN IN ARTS FESTIVAL

Students, faculty, and parents from MBA and Harpeth Hall are working diligently in preparation for our first Arts Festival. With the most appropriate title of Composition: Red and Green, the Arts Festival will include a variety of art forms for students and parents to enjoy.

On Tuesday, April 15, at 7:30 p.m. the choruses of the two schools will perform in Wallace Hall on the MBA campus. The program will include numbers by each group separately as well as some works done together. Following the choral performance, everyone is invited to the Patrick Wilson Library for a reception and an art show of student works. Students from both Harpeth Hall and MBA have worked diligently to prepare for this art show. During the reception, other students will be providing musical entertainment.

On Friday, April 18, MBA students will be bussed and "carred" to the Harpeth Hall campus at 12:30 for a box lunch on the lawn, followed by a program of student entertainment ranging from the Harpeth Hall Mime and Harpeth Pops groups to some MBA Rock bands. On Friday and Saturday evenings, Arsenic and Old Lace will be given in the beautiful new Davis Auditorium on the Harpeth Hall campus at 7:30 p.m. The cast includes a number of MBA students.

We hope that parents will make a special point to attend the evening events on Tuesday, April 15, and Friday or Saturday, April 18 and 19. Composition: Red and Green will be a success with your attendance.

MBA News and Views
March 1980
Publication from the 1970s
and 1980s to cummunicate
with parents and alumni

BY THESE PRESENTS BE IT KNOWN THAT THE
BOARD OF REGENTS OF THE
CVM LAVDE SOCIETY
HAS AUTHORIZED

MONTGOMERY BELL ACADEMY

Gordon E. Bondurant   Donald M. Fairbairn

Harold C. Crowell   G. Edward Gaffney

Joe C. Davis   Virginia M. Hollins

T. Michael Drake   Mary Helen Lowry

John E. Sloan

TO FOVND IN MONTGOMERY BELL ACADEMY
A CHAPTER OF THE SOCIETY TO BE CALLED
MONTGOMERY BELL CHAPTER
GIVEN VNDER OVR HANDS AND THE SEAL OF
THE SOCIETY THIS   14TH   DAY OF APRIL
MCMLXXXI

Wyatt Garfield
PRESIDENT GENERAL

Hubert B. Moore
SECRETARY GENERAL

Cum Laude Chapter
Established
1981

Gil Lackey, Class of 1984

I was afeared of her ages before she had me raking leaves on The Hill to work off her demerits. The legend of June Bowen, militaristic seventh grade English teacher, had preceded her.

But the truth behind Mrs. Bowen turned out to be more complex than the folklore. She was tough and fair and intimidating and hilarious. With her infamous in-class grammar contests, she fostered competition and a demand for perfection. I vividly recall diagramming sentences in my restless sleep (hopefully not while in her class).

Because of Mrs. Bowen I can't help but cringe when I hear the split infinitive at the beginning of each *Star Trek* episode, "To boldly go where no man has gone before." That is just poor grammar up with which I will not put!

But Mrs. Bowen didn't just cultivate lifelong grammarians. She mass-produced proper grammarians. Yes, Mrs. Bowen's discipline ushered me to demerit hall on many a Saturday. There, I learned a myriad of didactic vocabulary words but mostly just raked a boatload of leaves.

Many years later, I broke free from the bondage of school, teachers, parents, bosses, or any authority whatsoever. Yes, I purchased my own house.

As I strolled to the mailbox on that first autonomous day, my next-door neighbor introduced herself. "Welcome to the neighborhood. I'm June."

Holy moly, it was Mrs. Bowen! If I yawned without covering my mouth or left my shirttail hanging out, would I once again be relegated to raking leaves on Saturday? I felt that familiar shiver of afearedness!

On the contrary, Mrs. Bowen (no way I was calling her "June") turned out to be a dear friend and extraordinary neighbor. She probably hadn't changed much since I was in seventh grade, but 20 years had changed my perception of her. She was brilliant and witty and sarcastic and wonderful.

She called on me for small favors every once in a while, so I wasn't surprised when I saw her name on the caller ID that day. I agreed to come over to help her with a diagram. Only after I got off the phone did the terror hit me. A diagram? Are you kidding me? The lady wrote the book on diagramming sentences. That's not an idiomatic expression—I mean she literally wrote grammar books. I hadn't had fitful dreams about diagramming in 20 years, so how in the world could I not look the fool? This time, she really, really afeared me!

I searched in vain for my old "Rulebook" to jar my grammatical memory before fretfully knocking on her door. As I crept into her living room, I saw ceiling fan parts strewn about the floor. Next to the clutter, you may have guessed, were the ceiling fan instructions in the form of a diagram.

I have never been so relieved and overjoyed to put together a ceiling fan in all my life. I filled her in on the diagram miscommunication, and we both belly-laughed until tears ran down our faces.

These days, I envision Mrs. Bowen, red pen in hand, sending even the finest souls to rake leaves on an even bigger hill in Heaven. I also fancy thinking she would be pleased with the way she influenced my life. Although I graduated Mrs. Bowen's course with flying mediocrity, I think I have applied more of what I learned in that class than any other.

I married another hopeless grammarian and enjoy a career as an outdoor writer and editor. I have my own red pen, although it's in the form of a computer editing tool. I daily use a superfluity of didactic vocabulary words. And there are plenty of leaves to rake outdoors. But I must confess, she still afears me a little.

John Carter, Class of 1984

My years at MBA were transformative. The school's extraordinary academic environment honed me for college and set the standard of excellence for my life. MBA is undoubtedly one of the best schools in the country, and I am lucky to have had the opportunity to be a student there.

"THE ART OF TEACHING IS THE ART OF ASSISTING DISCOVERY."
—Mark Van Doren

MBA vs. Overton
1982
First game played
in the new football
stadium, later named
in 1991 for longtime
coach Tommy Owen

Campus Expansion
January 1982
Proposed Massey Junior School Building, new athletic facilities, a new science laboratory in the gym, and a newly renovated Carter Building
Left to right: De Thompson (Class of 1964), Pat Wilson (Wallace Class of 1937), Joe Davis (Class of 1937), Bronson Ingram (Class of 1949), Ben Gambill (Class of 1963).

Game Football
October 18, 1985.
MBA played Overton and won 54–0.
Inscribed by Coach Owen on the ball: 85-8 (for the 8th game in the
regular season). From this team, 1986 class members Robby Bueno
went on to play football at Yale and Jay Owen at Air Force Academy.

"OUR OWN HEART, AND NOT OTHER MEN'S OPINIONS, FORM OUR TRUE HONOR."
—Samuel Taylor Coleridge

Speech and Debate
Coach Billy Tate
1985

Reuben A. Bueno Jr. MD, Class of 1986

What do I remember about my experiences at MBA? I remember the work. It was the expectation then and is now. The five-paragraph themes, knowing the proper declension, no penalties for illegal motion, writing down the honor code on the lines of notebook paper folded vertically in half, making sure there were enough volunteers for the soup kitchen Saturday morning, cleaning up after basketball games—it was about the work for me. There was a sense of satisfaction and accomplishment in doing the work, but there was also joy in the effort. Perhaps the most important lesson that the teachers taught us was this: you earn what you get at MBA. Being held accountable for what you do is a lesson that even the youngest student at MBA can appreciate. Celebrating success is a wonderful thing, but just as important is the wisdom that comes from loss, disappointment, and failure. Looking back 30 years, I remember all those things as part of life on The Hill.

What has MBA meant to me as a graduate? I have met and worked with more people who know nothing of MBA and its history and tradition than those who do. I am sure I am not alone in that experience. For most people, their interaction with the school is only through one of its graduates and how that graduate treats them and others. My hope would be that all MBA graduates treat others with respect, with honor, and with kindness.

I had a richly rewarding experience at MBA as a student and as a teacher and coach. To me, the lasting impact of the school goes far beyond test scores, state championships, and college placement. I believe its greatest impact is in instilling values that provide the foundation for a meaningful life and in exposing boys to a worldview that allows them to serve others with respect, honor, and kindness. I will always be proud of my association with MBA, its teachers, and what the school represents.

"EVERY SCIENCE BEGINS AS PHILOSOPHY AND ENDS AS ART."
—Will Durant

Service Projects

Since its beginning, the MBA Service Club has expanded its range of duty and purpose enormously. Its mission has evolved from in-school projects to funded projects that require hundreds of hours from MBA students. This student-run organization seeks to extend the MBA community beyond the scope of the school. The group performs projects both to give back to the larger Nashville community and to raise revenue for the school itself. Working outside of the MBA community benefits students by allowing them to give of themselves and experience the value of community service. The Service Club will forever be evolving, as it continually searches for new projects to increase its impact on both the community and school.

Service Club

1986 Convention Center Opens
Photo credit: David Ewing

1980 TPAC
Photo credit: Tennessee Performing Arts

1985 Saturn Assembly Plant in Spring Hill
Photo credit: Chattanooga Times Free Press

1983 Riverfront Park Built
Photo credit: Tourism Media

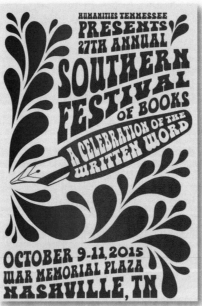

1988 Inaugural Southern Festival of Books
Photo credit: Humanities Tennessee

CHAPTER 6

1988–1994

Ridley Wills II, Frances Bond Davis, and Dr. Douglas Paschall
1992
Breaking ground for the Davis Building, named in honor of
Joe C. Davis, MBA's Board Chairman from 1979 to 1988

In 1988 MBA Board Chairman Joe Davis announced the trustees had selected Douglas Paschall to become the head-master, a position he held until 1994. This era witnessed increased enrollment, new buildings, and a greater focus on the arts and academics.

Aerial View of the Campus
1992

Robin Williams, meet Dr. Sam Pickering, Jr.

GENE WYATT

Robin Williams was the logical choice to play the antic prep school English teacher in *Dead Poets Society*, Disney's surprise summer movie hit.

But he should have had a character session with Sam Pickering, Jr., Ph.D., late of Nashville and now professor of English of the University of Connecticut.

Tom Schulman, a Nashville native and graduate of Montgomery Bell Academy, wrote the screenplay. It called for John Keating, the teacher, to outrage his peers by prancing around on a desk while delivering his rare lectures.

"It gives a different perspective," he explained, and he encouraged his students to do likewise.

Classes are taken outdoors for no particular reason. Most of all, he urges his charges to ignore the senseless pedantry of traditional textbooks, to the extent of tearing out offensive chapters.

Keating himself is a preppy who went on to college and "finished off" in England at Oxford. He comes back, filled with zeal, to his alma mater.

When Tom Schulman was a sophomore at MBA, his English class was taught by Pickering, who had gone to MBA, moved on to Vanderbilt and Sewanee, and "finished off" at Cambridge in England.

Back at his Harding Road alma mater, he lectured while seated on his desk, legs crossed, and urged his students to challenge everything. Occasionally he walked around with his feet in a wastebasket, and presided over classes with his back to his students. Sometimes, he even stood outside and conducted classes through the window.

He also inspired remarkable academic achievement.

Pickering hasn't gotten around to seeing the movie.

"I'm not avoiding it, but I have three small children, all with chicken pox. There aren't any first run theaters around (the University is at Storrs, in the Northeast part of the state). It's showing at a drive-in, but 47-year-old men with Plymouth station wagons and three sickly kids don't usually go there.

"I'm looking forward to seeing it, and if I recognize myself, I might just stand up and say 'that's me!' Maybe I'll ask them to stop the film and let me study it, but they might not understand."

Pickering has fond memories of his MBA teaching year. "I think they were a little puzzled by me. Bill Weaver once told me he heard that Nick Carter (the headmaster) would go home shaking his head and reporting that 'Sam was sitting on his desk again today.' But there certainly was never a confrontation such as I understand occurs in the movie.

"I remember the sophomore class that year very well. Such a great bunch of kids! Tommy Schulman, of course, and Gus Kuhn, and Steve Neff — all about as bright as you get."

Schulman worked around Nashville film operations a while. He has been in Los Angeles for a number of years, mostly writing. Neff is teaching law at the University of Edinburgh in Scotland. Gus Kuhn, now a Nashville toymaker, has nothing but good memories of Pickering.

"He was such an inspiration! He really wanted us to think, to find our own voice. It's interesting that I never knew his political orientation — he just wanted us to find our own way.

"I recognize some of the techniques in the movie. When we were studying Poe's *The Raven*, he had one boy stand on a chair. Every time we came to 'nevermore,' he flapped his arms like wings."

Schulman acknowledges his debt to Pickering. "Remember, I was 15 years old at the time. A lot of my love for the language and literature comes from that sophomore class. But there were other good teachers, at MBA and elsewhere. I owe a lot to Mrs. (Mary Helen) Lowrey particularly. She was a little eccentric herself, I guess, but nothing like Sam Pickering. She is a marvelous teacher — such an inspiration to me in my later years at MBA."

Weaver (William III) did not attend MBA but was a roommate of Pickering during his Sewanee years. "When I saw the movie, I couldn't believe it. It was Sam! I called him and told him it was the greatest tribute I could imagine."

Pickering has mellowed a bit over the years, even if his Connect-icut style occasionally lapses into the unorthodox. "Last Halloween, I tried teaching in a mask, but it didn't work out. People couldn't hear me. At the last class session of the fall semester, two girls came up and gave an imitation of my teaching style — crawling over desks and such like. It was good; they both got A's.

"One thing has changed. I no longer go outside and lecture through the window. My classroom is on the second floor now. It could be dangerous.

"If I have a teaching philosophy, I guess it would have to be that I want my students to challenge all the givens — not reject them, just challenge."

It has been a good year for Tom Schulman. In addition to *Dead Poets* he did the rewrite for *Honey, I Shrunk the Kids*, opening tomorrow. Both pictures likely will be very profitable. (The *New York Times* yesterday quoted Hollywood sources as saying that *Poets* likely would top $100 million in receipts.)

Pickering, who has published several novels and collections of essays, wishes his former student well.

"I earned the magnificent sum of $1,407 dollars from my writings last year. I hope Tommy does better."

He will. ∎

Tom Schulman, as a student at Montgomery Bell Academy in the 1960s.

Sam Pickering, Jr., today — an English professor at the University of Connecticut.

Sam Pickering sits on his desk to demonstrate his teaching style at Montgomery Bell Academy. Picture from an MBA yearbook.

Robin Williams, Meet Dr. Sam Pickering, Jr.
June 22, 1989
Newspaper article about the movie *Dead Poets Society*

Faculty Members Andy
Gaither and Anne Christeson
1990
Coaching track

"A TEACHER AFFECTS ETERNITY; HE CAN
NEVER TELL WHERE HIS INFLUENCE STOPS."
—Henry B. Adams

Banner file photo by Laura Embry

MBA pitcher R.A. Dickey has been named the Banner's All-Area Baseball Player of the Year.

Dickey: 'Wish I worked harder'

By Greg Pogue
Banner Sports Writer

6/8/43

ALL-AREA
BASEBALL

RELATED STORY
■ Forehand keeps battling, E-3

Believe it or not, R.A. Dickey has a few regrets about his days at Montgomery Bell Academy.

It might be hard to figure, too, because all Dickey did was lead the Big Red to a Class AAA state championship, be named the state's player of the year and, today, be named the *Nashville Banner* Area Player of the Year.

Last Thursday, he was selected in the 10th round of the Major League Baseball June amateur draft by the Detroit Tigers. He also has signed to play collegiately at the University of Tennessee.

What more could you ask for?

"I know it may sound corny," he said, "but I wish that I had worked even harder, stayed that extra hour or two to work on the things in sports that I needed to improve."

But it goes further than that.

"I don't think I would have said this when I began going to MBA in the seventh grade," he said, "but I wish I would have worked harder in school. I was involved in a lot of things and my grades are OK.

"But if kids were to come up to me and ask me what I would have done differently, it would have been to study harder and better prepare myself for the world."

Dickey's realm of reality,

Please see DICKEY, page E-3

R.A. Dickey, Class of 1993
June 8, 1993
Newspaper article about
Dickey's baseball career at
MBA

Dead Poets Society

In 1989 Tom Schulman, Class of 1968, received an Oscar for best screenplay for the film *Dead Poets Society*, starring Robin Williams. Schulman based the lead role on Sam Pickering Jr., who was his sophomore English teacher. The movie was an instant Hollywood classic, and the MBA lecture hall in Lowry Hall is named "Dead Poets Society Room" in honor of the film.

Dead Poets Society Statue
1998
Designed and created by Nashville sculptor Alan LeQuire, Class of 1974, the statue commemorates the movie *Dead Poets Society*, written by Tom Schulman, Class of 1968, in celebration of one of his MBA teachers, Sam Pickering Jr.

Montgomery Bell Academy

Celebrates the Holidays

Vine Street Christian Church

December 9, 1991

7:30 p.m.

Holiday Concert Program at
Vine Street Christian Church
December 9, 1991

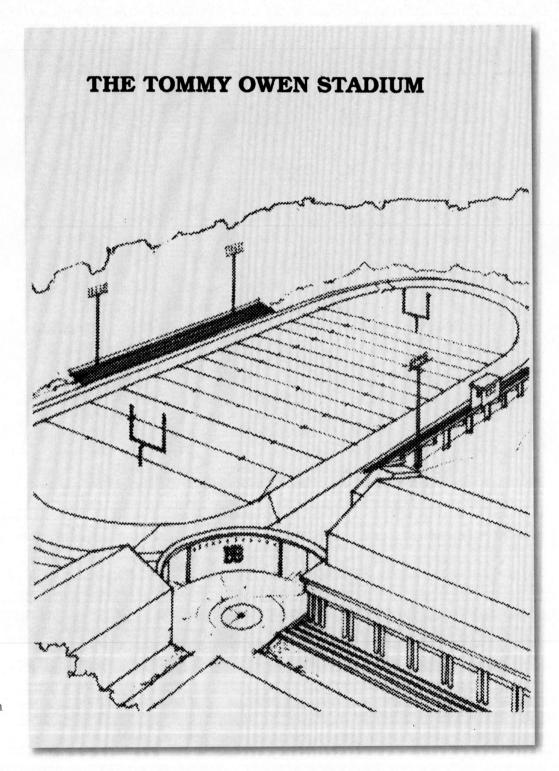

THE TOMMY OWEN STADIUM

Invitation to the Dedication
of Tommy Owen Stadium
September 13, 1991

Play Poster for *King Lear*
March 3–6, 1994

Reflections on Our School

Mauro M. Mastrapasqua, Class of 1990

For me, as I suspect for many of us alums, MBA is far more than a typical high school experience. I think the average person thinks of high school and either wants to forget that time entirely or wants to remain an active participant in the high school mindset. Our feelings are quite different, though. As involved as I have been with MBA since graduating 25 years ago, it is not because I desire to relive my high school years or because I particularly revel in asking for Annual Fund donations. The truth is, I enjoy remaining fully connected with my classmates and learning of the interesting developments in their lives. MBA has made me feel genuinely welcome as an alum, truly valuing my relationship with the school a quarter of a century later. I always desire to share that same welcome and sense of community with my class.

The MBA experience has followed me further into adulthood than I ever would have imagined. I did not realize at the time that the MBA ideal of "Gentleman. Scholar. Athlete" would grow in relevance as I aged. Brilliantly crafted, those three simple words carry the profound weight of a lifelong search for truth. It is remarkable how much meaning is packed into three words. The fact that it remains an ideal, something to be continually sought, yet never fully achieved, keeps it alive and vibrant to me today.

Twenty-five years ago, the ideal felt like it was about "yes ma'am" and "no ma'am," getting an A on the next test, and winning the next sporting event. Today, it is about being a civilized, sensitive, and well-mannered man, being kind to others above all else. It is about seeking knowledge, excellence, and ultimately truth in all I endeavor. And it is about working with those around me toward a common goal.

How timeless are the values that this institution instilled. Three simple words, ecumenical in nature, transcend all differences among us. College and graduate school taught me much about how life IS, but MBA taught me much about how life SHOULD be.

Faculty Member Dr. Jon Neergaard
1993
performing in assembly

MBA THEATRE in association with The Civil War Chess Set Presents

A 20th Century Classic

a tramp
a friend
a master
a slave
a boy
are all

WAITING FOR GODOT

by Samuel Beckett

with Paul Thompson,
Bill Siesser, Will O'Hare,
Andrew Vahrenkamp, and
Michael Martin

directed by
Bart Whiteman

Davis Building Theatre
February 18-20 at 8:00 p.m.
Tickets $6.00

4001 Harding Road
February 21 at 3:00 p.m.
Reservations:
298-5514 or 352-3418

Play Program for
Waiting for Godot
February 18–20, 1993

Visual and Performing Arts

MBA has a long tradition of excellence in the arts. Today the school fields strong programs in music, theater, drawing, watercolors, and sculpture. Activities outside of school are encouraged as well: the annual state Shakespeare competition, art exhibitions and competitions, and collaborative theater productions with MBA's sister school, Harpeth Hall.

1994 AT&T Building (Formerly Bell South)
Built
Public Domain

1990 Grassmere Wildlife Park (Now the Nashville Zoo)
Photo credit: Nashville Zoo

Tennessean Al Gore, 45th Vice-President of the U.S.
Public Domain

1989 Nashville Scene Begins Publication
Photo credit: Nashville Scene Magazine

Chapter 7

1994–Present

Long Mountain Observatory
2011

The modern era of MBA started on July 1, 1994, when Headmaster Brad Gioia was hired by the MBA Board. During this period MBA increased its academic strength with partnerships and exchanges with many international schools and Wilson Grants, providing opportunities and summer experiences across the globe. During this era the physical campus saw great improvement, including construction of a new dining hall, Ingram Science Building, and Lowry Hall. In addition the Ball, Massey, and Davis Buildings and the Wilson Library all were renovated. MBA purchased land in neighboring Sylvan Park for practice fields for sports, a mansion, and 150 acres on the Long Mountain Campus featuring an observatory. The campus footprint was expanded with the purchase of homes along MBA's eastern and southern borders and a new soccer field on top of a parking garage.

Ingram Science Building
1999

Students on an MBA
Summer Trip
1997

"THE MAN WHO DOES NOT READ GOOD BOOKS HAS NO
ADVANTAGE OVER THE MAN WHO CAN'T READ THEM."
—Mark Twain

Since 1994 MBA has enjoyed a number of physical changes on its campus, as well as increased its property by almost 225 acres. In 1996, through the generosity of the Wilson family, MBA gutted and renovated the Patrick Wilson Library in entirety and added 4,000 square feet to the building for additional space and study areas. Beginning in 2000, a major transformation occurred at the Harding Road campus through the development of a new front entrance, the building of the Ingram Science Building, the additions to the Massey Building, the rebuilding of the Carter Building, and the renovation of the lower level of the gymnasium for fitness and locker room areas. In 2004 MBA was given almost 200 acres of property at Long Mountain. The school currently enjoys a five-acre lake, hiking trails, two fields, an observatory, and low ropes and high ropes courses that were subsequently built. Also in 2004, the school purchased 10 acres of property at 42nd Avenue, which has been used primarily for playing fields over the past decade. Another significant transformation occurred in 2012 and 2013 when the school completed the purchase of 10 acres and 15 houses on Brighton Road and negotiated with both the city and the neighborhood to fold that property into the MBA campus so that the school could build an internal road as well as new tennis courts at the south end of campus. In 2012, MBA built a new parking garage with a soccer field on top,

the Rochford Rifle Center, and a maintenance area. In 2013, MBA built the new Lowry Building, which houses the English and math classes, a debate center, the Dead Poets Society Lecture Hall, a student center, and a new technology area. In 2013, the school finished this phase of construction by building the dining hall with history classrooms on the second floor. This dining area is in the central building on the campus. In the past four years MBA completed a major renovation of the art area in the Davis Building, redid the entrance and lobby areas of the Massey Building, built a new student center in the Junior School, and replaced the turf on the Rascoe Bond Davis football field. In 2017 MBA purchased approximately four acres from the Vine Street Christian Church, and this additional land adjoins the property of two houses on Ensworth Avenue the school had purchased in 1996 and 2014.

Perhaps more significant than all of these physical changes, MBA added over 200 students in grades seven through twelve, from approximately 542 to 750 students between the years 1994 and 2017. Of course the faculty and staff population grew proportionately, from approximately 90 faculty and staff to 140 faculty and staff, in that same period of time. The growth mirrors the changes in Nashville and the city's population, both in scope and diversity. The school has seen tremendous changes in a number of the extracurricular areas, especially music, theater, debate, art, robotics, and programs like Mock Trial and service. Our athletic teams have grown in scope and number, most significantly through the addition of crew and hockey. Signature programs that make the MBA experience both unique and profound are our Warner Exchanges and the Wilson Grants. Both programs provide extraordinary opportunities for our students to travel around the United States and the world. Literally hundreds of students benefit from these opportunities annually, and MBA has one of the largest exchange programs of all independent schools, with partner schools on six continents. MBA also provides almost $700,000 in Wilson Grants each year for its students.

Finally one of the most significant additions in this time period has been the depth and the development and importance of the advisory program. Students meet each day with faculty before school so that they are better known and cared for. This ritual is ingrained in both the routines and culture of the school. All the student body and faculty work hard to know one another better and more intimately.

"From what we get, we can make a living;
what we give, however, makes a life."
—Arthur Ashe

Commencement and Project Graduation

Project Graduation was started almost 30 years ago by a group of concerned parents who wanted to offer a safe, alcohol-free, and drug-free environment for students to celebrate graduation after a tragic accident involving an MBA senior. This annual event usually has every member of the senior class participating off campus in a facility that is rented exclusively for MBA. MBA faculty and senior parents help chaperone the popular all-night event.

Project Graduation Frisbee
2014

Nashville's Frank honored

MBA recognizes guide dog pioneer

By Katharine Mosher
kmosher@nashvillecitypaper.com

Morris Frank, father of the Seeing-Eye dog movement in the United States, will be remembered Monday at his alma mater, Montgomery Bell Academy, with a play about his life story.

Two separate childhood accidents claimed Frank's eyes, but he overcame blindness and opened the door for other visually-impaired Americans to live more a more independent life.

Frank found his ticket to freedom in a 1927 *Saturday Evening Post* article about shepherd dogs trained to help World War I veterans.

Reporter Dorothy Eustis gave him $10,000 to bring the technique to the United States.

Frank founded The Seeing Eye in Nashville two years later.

Actor Bill Mooney will present the play *With a Dog's Eyes: Capturing The Life of Morris Frank* at 7 p.m. Monday.

Tickets are $15 for the play or $25 to include dinner at 6 p.m. All proceeds benefit The Seeing Eye, now located in Morristown, N.J.

Photo courtesy of Montgomery Bell Academy

Nashville native Morris Frank and his Seeing-Eye dog, photographed in 1938, logged thousands of miles giving hope to vision-impaired people.

Morris Frank, Class of 1924
January 28, 2005
Newspaper article about play honoring Morris Frank, father of the seeing-eye dog movement in the U.S.

Coat Drive
2015
Annual drive benefitting the
Nashville Rescue Mission

Patrick Wilson
Library Poster
2013
Promoting mobile
access to the MBA
library

Glass Recycling Service Project
2015
Partnering with Justice Industries
to employ Nashville workers

Ryan Hill, Class of 2011

Aside from my own wedding, perhaps the most jubilant afternoon of life so far was the day our Big Red Varsity Cross-Country Team claimed its second consecutive state title in the fall of 2011. Our audience at the racecourse was actually similar in nature to the guest list for a wedding. Separate communities of people with nothing in common but the family of honor came together for one joyous celebration. Our team, like any couple moving toward its big day, had many opportunities for bonding that season across hundreds of miles in Warner Park long runs, Centennial Park tempos, and track repeats on The Hill. Nothing else galvanized us, though, quite like the climactic 20 minutes on that mild, sunny, wind-swept October day.

The race itself makes up little of the memory. Those seconds of teetering over the line before a starter's gun sounds are endless. The five kilometers themselves are over in a flash of sweat, footfalls, and lactic acid. Sweeping the top five positions as we crossed the finish line, a rare move earning us the lowest score possible of 15 points at a cross-country meet, was fun to brag about for months. What I smile about years later is the unlikely mix of celebrants who met us just across the line.

Proud parents, siblings, and extended family. Giddy coaches, not typically prone to outbursts, slapping backs and whooping. Fellow Big Red boys from honors classes, regular classes, the theater crew, the debate team. The biggest surprise was some huge fraction of the football team. Dominant on the field in our day, they showed up at the meet to pay a tribute that was miles beyond lip service. Those stocky young men sporting bandanas and hand-painted cut-offs waved maroon flags the size of tables above our starting line and blew vuvuzelas as the race exploded into action. As harrier after harrier finished his race, they swept up the much skinnier boys wearing singlet tops and skimpy shorts and just about force-fed them the delights of home-grilled bratwurst and honeybuns fresh from the package then fried in butter. How they transported propane tanks, cast iron skillets, and several grills to the infield of our course (better known as the Steeplechase) is beyond me.

This picture of acceptance inspires me today and characterizes MBA at its best. The fanfare we received was plain gratuitous. Our perfect score at the state meet sounds more momentous than it was. We competed in a small division with other private schools and would have stood a much tougher test racing area public schools. In terms of mass appeal, cross-country will never compete with football. Still, those football players—free just to bask in their own dominance, to smile over their empire—turned out *en masse* to serve us for the afternoon, to feed us, to make us feel like kings of the world. What a perfect picture of humility: people with power taking themselves out of the spotlight and using that power to encourage, to celebrate, to lift up others. I am thankful to my classmates for this example. Roll Red!

Students Paint Up
for Football
2013

Football State Champions
2014
Bumper sticker

College T-shirt Day

Each May, on the last day before exams, seniors proudly wear t-shirts from their chosen colleges. With a rigorous curriculum, MBA students prove year after year that they can compete with the best and brightest across the country. MBA's dress code requires that students wear a shirt with a collar, but on this day of celebration of continuing their education, students wear a wide range of colors with college names, nicknames, and mascots from schools all over the country.

College T-shirt Day
2013

Summer Sports Camps

The Hill comes alive during the summer when students from MBA and numerous area schools are on campus for a series of sports camps. These week-long camps offer further instruction and competition in sports like basketball, baseball, golf, football, lacrosse, soccer, rowing, rifle, tennis, wrestling, and other activities. Many future MBA students first experience the campus during these popular camps which provide fun and competition for a variety of sports.

Summer Sports Camps
2012
Brochure

2012 Sports Camps
www.montgomerybell.edu/camps

"I'M ACTUALLY AS PROUD OF THE THINGS WE HAVEN'T DONE AS THE THINGS I HAVE DONE. INNOVATION IS SAYING NO TO 1,000 THINGS."

—Steve Jobs

Big Red Spirit Bus
2006
For varsity football games

Ingle Martin, Class of 2001

MBA is a special place for many reasons, including all the ones that people see in academics, athletics, or community service. But the most outstanding piece to what separates MBA has been the people that have walked the hallways or taught in the class-rooms. The relationships that are built at MBA liter-ally last a lifetime. For me as a boy growing up and maturing while on campus, the teachers and coaches that I had as well as my classmates are owed all the credit for the quality of my experience. They men-tored me, they pushed me, they made me laugh, and made me want to cry (English themes or physics tests!). MBA has been and will always be one of the nation's leading schools when it comes to educating boys due to the fact that its first priority is the people that work and learn there. I am forever grateful for MBA's impact on my life.

"I HAVE A DREAM THAT ONE DAY THIS NATION WILL RISE UP AND LIVE OUT THE TRUE MEANING OF ITS CREED: 'WE HOLD THESE TRUTHS TO BE SELF-EVIDENT, THAT ALL MEN ARE CREATED EQUAL.'"

—Martin Luther King Jr.

Microbe Cross-Country Warms Up in the Runners' Grove
2013

Freshman at the Ocoee River
2013
Annual trip before school begins

International Boys School Student Conference at MBA
June 2014

Crew in Action
2013

Debate Honors
2017
#1 in the U.S. policy
debaters Andrew Kaplan
and Ben Rosenthal

13th Consecutive HVAC Soccer Championship
2015

Building Boys into Better Men

Montgomery Bell Academy is a school where boys are taught the value of leadership and character; are equipped with the fundamental tools to succeed in the classroom and beyond; develop an appreciation for the effort required to achieve excellence; and form friendships that last a lifetime.

Facts & Figures

- Student body of 755 in grades 7-12
- Entering students represent 37 different public and private schools
- 7:1 student-teacher ratio
- 21 percent of student body receive more than $2 million in need-based financial aid
- 68 percent of faculty hold advanced degrees, including 13 doctorates
- 18 National Merit Finalists; 12 Commended Scholars; and 16 National AP Scholars in 2015/16
- Average ACT scores were 8 points higher than the national average in 2015
- 27 AP classes offered
- 4 national championships in debate, including Novice and Middle School Champs in 2015
- Active community service leadership: soup kitchen, peer tutoring, Race for the Cure, and Time to Rise
- 5 Theater state championships since 2005
- 200-plus acre campus on Long Mountain near McMinnville, Tennessee with an observatory
- Field space exclusively for Junior School athletics on 42nd Avenue in Sylvan Park
- State championships in basketball, cross-country, football, lacrosse, rifle, soccer, swimming, and tennis over the last decade, including football and soccer in 2014-15
- This past summer, MBA sent more than 60 high-school students on service and educational programs spanning the globe – all at the school's expense.
- Wilson and college grants sent more than 125 students to national and international programs in 2016.
- The Warner International Exchange program sent another 26 juniors on cultural and academic exchanges to programs in the United Kingdom, Colombia, China, Singapore, South Africa, New Zealand, and Australia.
- 2015/16 HVAC All-sports Championship for Middle School

ADMISSION PREVIEW DAY

Sunday, October 30 @ 2 p.m.

4001 HARDING ROAD • NASHVILLE, TN 37205 • 615-369-5316
WWW.MONTGOMERYBELL.EDU

Admission Preview Day
2015

MBA Fall Art Show

PRESENTED BY THE 2011-2012 MBA MOTHER'S CLUB

ART BY KIM BARRICK "ASPEN DANCE"

August 30 *to* September 30

MBA Campus
Davis Theater and
The Gibbs Room

Opening Reception
Tuesday, August 30, 2011
5:30 - 7:30 pm

Free to the public.
A portion of all proceeds to benefit
Race for the Cure

Artists

Beth Affolter
Christina Baker
Kim Barrick
Bebo
Leslee Bechtel
Mick Beisel
Anne Carter Brothers

Gordon Chenery
Jane Coble
Kelley Estes
Elizabeth Foster
Otis Goodin
Carey Haynes
Deann Herbert
Charlie Hunt
Paige Morehead

Kris Prunitsch
Jason Saunders
KJ Schumacher '97
Vicki Shipley
J.J. Sneed
Streater Spencer
Charlotte Terrell
Tom Turnbull
Ron York

MBA Art Show
2012

MBA Orchestra
2016

Exam Changes

Traditionally Northeastern colleges and boarding schools gave their first semester examinations in January after the December break. Harvard University changed this tradition of over 250 years in 2009. MBA students also now take their exams in December before the holiday break, a change made in 2008.

Founder's Day Race

A recent tradition at MBA is the the Founder's Day run, held on campus each spring. This event is named after MBA alum Vann Webb (Class of 2000), a member of the track team who passed away after a battle with cancer. The race around the Sloan Quadrangle in the campus in a Chariots-of-Fire-inspired competition finishes in front of the dining hall. The students run down a gauntlet of cheering students to the finish line.

Founder's Day Race

"EDUCATION IS THE MOST POWERFUL WEAPON
WHICH YOU CAN USE TO CHANGE THE WORLD."
—Nelson Mandela

Ring Day Ceremony, established in 1996

The MBA gold signet ring with the iconic waffle logo is worn by generations of MBA graduates. In a special ring day ceremony during the junior year, each student receives his gold school ring in front of his classmates.

Students at Martin Luther King Day March
2009
In downtown Nashville

Wilson Grants

David K. "Pat" Wilson's visionary and generous gift to MBA has already given hundreds of students the opportunity to further their studies in the United States and abroad in the areas of math, science, English, history, the arts, and language immersion. These annual grants awarded to MBA allow each student selected to receive up to $10,000 in travel grant opportunities for expanding their education and experiencing learning in a different environment. The legacy of Pat Wilson, a graduate of Wallace School Class of 1937 and former member of the MBA Board of Trustees, will continue for centuries through these special awards.

Warner Exchanges

Headmaster Brad Gioia initiated the exchange program in 1998 with Eton College in England. Programs were funded by Dudley Warner (Class of 1961) and his wife, Beth, through the Dudley Warner Foundation. Today's boys enjoy exchanges with schools in South Africa, England, New Zealand, Australia, China, Singapore, Columbia, Spain, Germany, France, and Argentina.

Advisory

To foster a student's growth and achievement as "gentleman, scholar, and athlete" in the MBA tradition, each student has an advisor to work closely with him, his teachers, coaches, activity supervisors, and parents. The primary role of the advisor is to encourage the advisee to realize his full potential in all aspects of MBA life, which includes guiding him in developing good study habits, assisting him in course selections, and helping him accept challenges and resolve difficulties as they arise. Consequently, the advisor confers with the advisee and acts as his advocate, providing guidance and direction, and coordinating efforts on his behalf with other teachers and with parents. Students meet briefly with their advisors each morning for attendance and announcements. This brief meeting, prior to first period, offers an opportunity for advisors to encourage students and arrange individual meetings as necessary. Meeting with the advisee to monitor his progress and to address his particular questions and concerns throughout the year, the advisor also reviews grades and teacher comments with him each mid-quarter and quarter.

1999 Adelphia Coliseum
Photo credit: Tennessee Titans

1996 Bridgestone Arena Opens
Photo credit: E. Vula

2001 Frist Center for Visual Arts
Photo credit: The Frist Center

2001 New Downtown Nashville Public Library
Opens
Photo credit: Robert A.M. Stern Architects

1998 Tennessee Oilers
Photo credit: The Sports
E-Cyclopedia

1998 Nashville Predators
Photo credit: Christopher Hanewinckel, *USA Today*

1998 Tornado Rips through Nashville
Photo credit: David M. Schwarz Architects

2010 Nashville Flood
Photo credit: Nashville Public Library
Digital Collections

2006 Schermerhorn Symphony Center
Photo credit: David M. Schwarz Architects

"ONE LIE DOES NOT COST YOU
ONE TRUTH, BUT THE TRUTH."
—Friedrich Hebbel

"WE ALL NEED SOMEONE
WHO INSPIRES US TO DO BETTER
THAN WE KNOW HOW."

—Anonymous

"ALL MEN BY NATURE
DESIRE TO KNOW."
—Aristotle

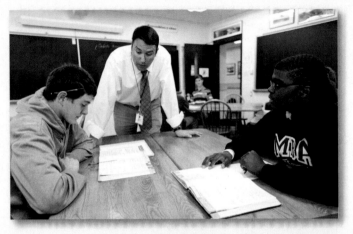

"REPUTATION IS WHAT OTHER PEOPLE KNOW
ABOUT YOU. HONOR IS WHAT YOU KNOW
ABOUT YOURSELF."

—Lois McMaster Bujold

"GREAT IS TRUTH AND MIGHTY ABOVE ALL THINGS."
—The Apocrypha 4:41

"SOME PEOPLE DRINK FROM THE FOUNTAIN OF
KNOWLEDGE; OTHERS JUST GARGLE."

—Robert Anthony

"WHEN WEALTH IS LOST,
NOTHING IS LOST.
WHEN HEALTH IS LOST,
SOMETHING IS LOST.
WHEN INTEGRITY IS LOST,
ALL IS LOST."

—German Proverb

"TRUTH IS THE SAFEST LIE."

—Yiddish Proverb

"THERE IS TRUE GLORY AND A TRUE HONOR:
THE GLORY OF DUTY DONE—THE HONOR
OF THE INTEGRITY OF PRINCIPLE."

—Robert E. Lee

"TO TELL A FALSEHOOD IS LIKE THE CUT OF A SABER; FOR THOUGH THE WOUND MAY HEAL, THE SCAR OF IT WILL REMAIN."

—Saadi

"SOMETIMES WE STARE SO LONG AT A DOOR
THAT IS CLOSING THAT WE SEE TOO LATE
THE ONE THAT IS OPEN."
—Alexander Graham Bell

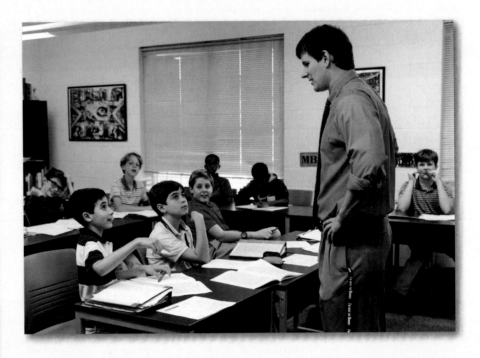

"Make us to choose the harder right instead of the easier wrong and never to be content with a half truth when the whole can be won."
—Cadet Prayer, U.S. Military Academy

"SCIENCE DOES NOT KNOW ITS
DEBT TO IMAGINATION."
—Ralph Waldo Emerson

INDEX

Joe C. Davis, Class of 1937
(Pictured on Far Right)
National Tennis Championship

The Joe Davis financial aid endowment has opened up opportunities at MBA for young men throughout middle Tennessee.

David K. "Pat" Wilson,
Wallace Class of 1937

The Wilson grants have given young men at MBA transformative opportunities around the world.

Dudley, Class of 1961, and Beth Warner

The Warner exchanges have transformed MBA with an international focus and dimension since 1998.